A Little Off the Top:

Stories of Haircuts, Barbers, and Barber Shops

Edited by Proal Heartwell

For all barbers everywhere

Acknowledgements

Thanks to Ed Roseberry for the cover photo of Charlottesville's Staples Barber Shop, circa 1960. Thanks, also, to Steve Trumbull and his efforts to preserve Ed's photographic legacy.

Introduction

I'm not entirely sure where the idea for this little book originated. I suspect it may have been at a friends's 60th birthday party (there have been a lot of those recently) when one guest described a recent barber shop visit gone awry. If so, then the obvious truth dawned on me: most guys have stories about haircuts, barbers, and barber shops.

With this axiom in mind and confronted with an extended summer reprieve from teaching, I emailed about forty friends proposing we each write a short essay about our own barber shop or haircut experiences. There were to be no "rules" as such, although I suggested submissions should be about 1,000 words. Of the twenty-two who met the challenge, most are my contemporaries, "men of a certain age." However, there is a chronological range among the writers, from age eleven to age seventy-four. Most of the writers also live in or have roots in Charlottesville, although a couple of contributors are boon companions of my long-ago youth. And, finally, a few of the authors are members of my extended family who no doubt felt obligated to participate for the sake of familial harmony.

I'd like to thank all those who contributed the stories you have in front of you. Additionally, I'd like to acknowledge those who did not send in pieces, but who, nonetheless, graciously put up with my barrage of hectoring email appeals.

A Little Off the Top has been a fun project start to finish, and I hope you will enjoy reading this anthology. All proceeds from the sale of this book will be donated to the Boys & Girls Club of Central Virginia.

Proal Heartwell

Table of Contents

The Unattended

by Bahlmann Abbot

Three brothers left at home with their dad for a long summer day sounds, on the surface, to be a reasonable arrangement. At least that is what my mother had counted on when she drove down to the state capital for the day to visit her parents. It was rare in those days, and for my parents' generation, to leave a father in charge of the children for any significant length of time. However my brothers and I were finally old enough that Dad wouldn't likely have to perform any distasteful tasks. If my memory serves me well, we were in the range of seven, six and three years old at the time. The only request my mother had made was for Dad to take us all to town for a haircut.

We lived just a mile outside the county seat of Fayette County, West Virginia and a drive up town took little more than five minutes. However sitting in the barber shop for the length of time it would take Mr. Hatcher to cut all our heads was more time than our restless dad wanted to spend listening to Hatcher's take on local politics. That's why Dad had recently enlisted our mom to cut his hair. She had invested in some new electric clippers and attachments for the purpose. The other problem Dad had with our town barber was the inability to convey to him what was a proper hair cut. Dad had gone to military school and had served in the army, and a hair cut was a practical matter. Mr. Hatcher would cut the hair short enough around the ears but he was fond of leaving it longer on top so that there was what Dad referred to as "wings" on either side of our head. Later on in life we suspected Mr. Hatcher had simply been following our mother's covert instructions.

So instead of taking us to town as he and Mom had discussed, Dad found the clippers and had us sit in a chair he pulled out in the yard. With his unlit stogie in the side of his mouth, one by one he carved at our unruly scalps. His old transistor radio was nearby on the porch rail and a ball game was on. I believe the Orioles were playing for a pennant. This was the other motivation for not taking us up to Hatcher's; he would miss some of the game.

When late afternoon rolled around and Dad had finished with us, I looked at my brothers and realized that there was mischief in the air. In his effort to give us a proper cut he had overcompensated. We no longer had the dreaded "wings;" in fact the only hair left with any length was a narrow strip starting at the forehead and ending at the back of our necks. Dad had tapped into his own well of creativity, and perhaps he was ahead of the times for we were the first kids I know of to have Mohawk-style haircuts. We ran in to the house to look in the mirror and soon after found any Indian style garments we had lying around. We spent the remainder of the afternoon building blanket teepees, making crude weapons, and engaging in battle. Dad even got in on the fun and died a gruesome death as the only cowboy.

All in all, I think Dad was pretty proud of himself but when the time approached for my mother's return we sensed a little apprehension in his mood. However, my brothers and I were excited to show our mother our new look and sat on the porch with Dad watching for the car in the driveway. When she finally arrived we dashed down to greet her. Dad waited tentatively on the porch. As he used to tell it, he thought he saw my mother smiling and laughing when she stepped out to find her little boys gone native. At least he said he could see her teeth. But as he approached the car he realized it was a grimace along with some tears. It would take until later that evening and some follow-up work with the clippers for Mom to finally laugh along. Of course we boys were disappointed, our days as native people cut short.

Years later when I had taken up residence in Charlottesville, Virginia, it was hard to find a regular barber shop. Out of necessity I found a walk-in salon near the University. There were no male barbers here; my new "stylist" was Tammy. Once when my parents were in town for a visit with the grandchildren, I went in to see Tammy to get cleaned up for the occasion. I sat down, making the usual small talk and heard a familiar voice say my name. Turning to my right there was my mother seated in the next chair getting her hair done. She had randomly found the very same salon. "I guess the times really have changed," she laughed.

I turned and asked Tammy if she could give me a Mohawk. "What color?" she replied.

Barbicide

by Cortlandt Schoonover

The boy didn't want to be there with his father in the barber shop, waiting for his first professional haircut. It seemed perfectly fine to do things the way they had always been done: his mother had a tool called a Flowby, which was a buzzer that attached to the vacuum cleaner. The vacuum's sucking action caused the blades to whirr, and the hair clippings were neatly contained.

That was what the boy knew. Sure it made a lot of noise, and sometimes he wondered if his ear could get caught in the Flowby, but it was what he had grown up with.

This shop was something different altogether. The striped pole had seemed innocuous enough—it reminded him of ice cream—but now that he was awaiting his turn in the waiting chairs, like a death-row inmate, he could only wish for a stay of execution before he had to climb up in one of the barber's chairs.

There was a jar behind the three barbers which had a neon-blue liquid in it. They kept dipping used combs into it and selecting new ones.

"Dad, what does that say?" he asked, pointing.

"Barbicide."

His father did not elaborate, and rather than let his mind come up with all the terrible ways Barbicide could be used, he returned his gaze to the magazine on his lap. He had picked this one because it had an image of a familiar football player on the cover. It was a small reprieve to be able to flip through and look at the different pictures.

There was a tennis player mid-swing.

A bunch of horses galloped toward the camera.

A woman stood at the edge of a diving platform, stretching upward. The background of the photo was a bright blue, like Barbicide. The boy flipped the page. He looked down the row of chairs, and noticed only two men were ahead of him in line.

"Dad, who will go first, you or me?"

"Well, since it's your first real man's haircut, I think you should go first, son."

The boy sighed. He looked at the other magazines in the rack: lots of men wearing camouflage, or holding guns, or both. In one there was a wetland of some sort, and a man holding a fishing pole. Another had a different football player that the boy didn't know on the cover. Several had cars or trucks on front, and one had a picture of a satellite.

The covers displaying trucks made the boy glance out the window to the shop's tiny six vehicle capacity parking lot. His dad's red truck seemed much smaller than some of the other customers' gargantuan pickups. One had four doors, and another had a huge shiny locked box in back.

The boy returned to his seat next to his father: there was only one man left in line now.

Each of the three barbers looked horrible in his own way. One had thick glasses, and had to press his face close to the customer to try to cut a straight line in his hair. Another had palsied hands, the scissors jumped and quivered as he brought them near to his victim's scalp.

The third was impossibly old. His wrinkles had wrinkles. His sunspots had sunspots. The hair coming out of his ears was longer than the hair on top of his head, but all of the hair was white. The boy was surprised at how much hair was on top of the barber's head. Was it possible that he wore a toupee? Were barbers allowed to? This eldest barber seemed to be the leader. The boy began thinking of nicknames for each of the three.

The one with shaky hands was easy—he was "The Butcher." The boy only had to look at the haircuts he gave to see that name was true. The bespectacled one was "Daredevil," and the captain was "Father Time."

If Father Time's hair wasn't a toupee, then who cut his hair? Clearly he cut The Butcher's and Daredevil's hair. It was like the picture from science class—the mouse ate the bug, the snake ate the mouse, and the eagle ate the snake. Father Time was the eagle. What eats the eagle? Surely Father Time didn't go to the barber shop across town where some of the boys from his school got their hair cut. The boy couldn't explain why it couldn't happen that way, but even as young as he was, he could feel that that was the way the world worked. There are divisions that people make that are as real as the walls of the barbershop.

(Later, when the boy would grow into the narrator, me, he would know how some of those divisions that kept the two shops separate were formed, but the 'why' would remain elusive. He would also know of something called the "Barber Paradox," which is about a barber who shaves all the men in town—and only those—who do not shave themselves. But—to quote Wikipedia—"Despite its popular name, however, barber paradox is not really a paradox in the true sense of this word. A man who shaves exactly those men who do not shave themselves simply cannot and does not exist, and there are virtually no reasons to expect the opposite. This is in contrast with the set of all sets that do not contain themselves (from Russell's paradox), whose existence cannot be painlessly dismissed as it follows from the very intuitive and widely relied upon axioms of naive set theory.")

During the period in which the boy was thinking into the future, Father Time had finished cutting a man's hair, and that man had given him twelve dollars, plus three additional dollars for the tip, and his chair was wide open, ready for the boy to sit in it and receive his cut.

But the customer leaving had accidentally left the door open, and it too beckoned.

Moonshine Haircuts

by Frank Kilgore

My WWII dad cut my hair to save the fifty cents. This was one of many vain reasons that I left home at age seventeen. For some reason, he didn't notice I needed a cut until he drank some of the moonshine he made in the steep woods behind the house. I found his copper "worm" inside an old coal mine opening one day while running the forests. I rolled it back to the house thinking we could straighten it out and use it for the perpetual but futile attempt to pipe water into our tiny house from a very intermittent spring. To the great surprise and dismay of my dad, Leo, our nosy neighbor and self-appointed mayor of Honey Branch, was visiting just as the tumbling copper coil, my six mongrel dogs, and I came bursting from the trees. But I digress.

Each haircut was unique and memorable, depending upon the quality of that particular run of homemade brew. When Pap was happy, I got the choppy trim which looked like zigzag plow furrows etched into a thick brown hedge. Or an outbreak of sporadic mange. When sad, he seemed to think a G.I. cut would man me up a little so I could face life with the right attitude. When he was angry, due to high octane headaches, the Mohawk was the certain choice.

Once he tried to carve my initials, "FK," into the short sidewalls, but the result was very gaped and garbled, embarrassingly so. Girls tried to guess the letters, the closest they ever got to me during my high school days. My male buddies had no problem filling in the letters they thought they saw.

Just like Johnny Cash, whose dad named him Sue, I had to fight my way through school and beyond. I give credit to my late father for making me tough and determined. Determined to hire a damn school-trained barber as soon as possible!

The Beauty Parlor

by Gary Moody

At 72 and hair challenged, I find I tend to spend more energy worrying about how I can retain order and presentation to what little supply of hair remains than recalling earlier times when a more ample and regenerative head of hair was willingly given over to the fate of someone else's interpretation of a good haircut. At the same time, however, I find myself reflecting more and more on the importance that hair has in many of our lives, an importance that seems to expand in proportion to diminishing natural production.

Most of us, especially when we are young, take for granted the rhythm of hair growth, haircuts, and hairstyle management having little or no concern or appreciation for the gift we have been given. We color it, shave it, shape it, iron it, grease it, bleach it, oil it, brush it, soak it in chemicals, and do all matter of other things to this glorious gift with a naïve confidence that no matter what we do, it will always continually populate and repopulate our heads with glorious locks that can somehow become subject to our whims and satisfaction. At some point, however, we are inevitably forced to present ourselves and our glorious head of hair quietly and submissively as a willing sacrifice to the interpretive elimination and shaping of the haircut gods.

As one of three boys in a family of five kids haircuts were generally done at home by my dad using whatever implements he had available. Initially, it was simply a pair of not so sharp scissors and a comb with little or no regard for the end product other than it being short and quick. In a matter of minutes, my dad could transform a beautiful, full head of curly and wavy hair into a display of stubble and irregularity leaving only the knowledge it would eventually grow out again only to become victim to a future desecration and destruction. Eventually, the addition of electric clippers with attachments that assured uniform hair length in less than one minute replaced painful dull scissors and reduced the mutilation to a more military and uniform look.

I can't recall my first visit to an official barber but can only assume that it was a welcome relief from the DIY experiences I had suffered under my dad's well-intentioned endeavors. However, somewhere along the way, it became clear to me that boys and men should only have their hair cut by male barbers unless it was an emergency and then only if done by a relative (like your mother, aunt or grandmother). Real men do not eat quiche and certainly do not go to a beauty salon to get a haircut.

After losing my regular barber to retirement and being less than satisfied with barber replacements, I was mortified when my wife casually suggested I go to her hair dresser to have my hair cut. My response insinuated that no man alive would be found dead getting his hair cut in a beauty salon to which she assured me there were at least two or three that her hair dresser cut all the time. I was busted but I needed a haircut and needed it bad.

After having my wife make the appointment, with great fear and trepidation I made my way to the dreaded beauty parlor. With my masculinity at stake, I walked through the door into a world I had never been before. There must have been what seemed to be over 100 women having their hair washed, curled, dyed, blow dried or put up in rollers with all sorts of horrific aromas that I had never experienced. I stood there in almost a frozen state, so confused and disoriented that I couldn't decide whether to run or just die. But then, almost from far away I heard someone call out my name and tell me they were ready for my 2:30 appointment. Almost like a zombie, I followed the voice deep into the bowels of this strange place where I was offered a seat as part of a group of people in which I was the only male. Trying to ignore my embarrassment and shame, I somehow stammered through questions concerning my haircut preferences and then just sat there looking straight ahead hoping for the whole ordeal to end as soon as possible having little or no concern for the process or end result. Afterwards, having somehow survived the incident I quickly made it to my car and adjusted my rear view mirror to examine the full extent of the damage. Turning my head from side to side and tipping it backward and forward I looked again and again at the results, with amazement and surprise.

Best haircut I had ever had and better yet she has been my barber ever since producing quality haircuts through thick and thin. However, even better than all of that, I still seem to have retained all my masculinity, if not my hair. Maybe, sometime, I will let my wife know how much I appreciate her suggestion.

The Shoeshine Man

by Francis Eugene Wood

I don't remember his name. Joe or James, maybe they called him Buck. That was a pretty common nickname back then. I knew several boys and men who went by that moniker.

It was the early 1960s. I mostly recall referring to him as the shoeshine man. He would show up two or three days during the week at the Main Street Barber Shop, the one owned and operated by Johnny Carpenter and Wilson Elmore in Lawrenceville, Virginia, the town where I grew up in the 1950s and 1960s. I moved away in 1971. But when I lived there, that little town was a bustling example of mid-twentieth century Americana. I mean, all of the storefronts were occupied by well-known merchants. I knew most of their names. My parents were friends with many of them. Some attended my church.

Friday afternoons in that little town were crazy. The sidewalks were crowded at times with shoppers moving from store to store. Traffic was a constant stream of cars and trucks that could be slowed to a snail's pace by a local plowman, whose mule-drawn wagon laden with plow and disc bridged the margin between the old days and the modern world as it squeaked and plodded along. There were no angry drivers lined up behind him. No horn blowing or racing engines. It was a usual occurrence in small town America then.

I always paused to see the plowmen pass by when I was a boy. And often times, it was while sitting at the window of the barbershop, waiting for my turn at a haircut and flipping through a variety of magazines, such as *Sports Illustrated*, *Field and Stream*, or *Life*, I might even pause during a game of checkers while the plowman went by. Most times, if possible, I would avoid sitting in those uncomfortable, heavy wire-back chairs. You know, the ones with the swirl right at the center of your back and the hard, wooden seat. I'd take the front window seat any day over that!

Johnny cut my hair most of the time. Not that there was much to it. I wore a crewcut until, thank God, the Beatles hit America and improved the stagnant variety in men's hair styles. I liked Johnny a lot. He had a real jovial personality, and he always seemed to know how to talk to kids. I was a shy boy, but he could always pull a little conversation from me.

Mr. Elmore was a good man, too. I let him cut my hair if Johnny had too many heads before me and I was in a hurry. The older barber was one of my Little League baseball coaches and the father of Rodney, a school chum of mine.

Now, often while I'd be waiting for my turn in the barber chair, the shoeshine man would be busy at his trade. It was mostly merchants and businessmen wearing neatly-pressed shirts and narrow ties who would pay fifty cents for a shine. But man, what a shine they'd get while they sat up there in that big chair like kings, reading newspapers, their feet resting on cast-iron footrests, their butts on a cushioned seat. The shoeshine chair at the Main Street Barber Shop sat high above a double-decker wood base and had a backrest and arms. It was old then, probably from the 1930s. I believe it was made of oak.

Sometimes I'd sit up there if the shoeshine man wasn't in, and no other kids beat me to the "throne." I liked the view of the shop from that height. But what I wanted was a shine on my Sunday shoes.

The cost for a shine was hard to come by for me then. I would see the men hand a dollar to the shoeshine man on occasion, and I knew it would be difficult for me to match that. But I was a determined boy when I set my sights on something. And one day I came to the barbershop with an extra hard-earned seventy-five cents in my pocket and wearing a pair of brown penny loafers.

After my dollar and twenty-five cents haircut, I walked over and took my seat upon the throne, where I quietly waited until the shoeshine man finally realized that I really wanted my shoes shined. I can see him now as he smeared on the Kiwi polish. He hit the sides of my soles with a darker goop and then commenced to brushing and buffing to beat the band! When he had finished, I handed him his fifty cents, paused to admire my shiny loafers, and then dropped him a quarter tip. It was worth every penny, too. Believe me. The shine on those loafers lasted for months. And the pride I felt when wearing them has stayed with me for years.

I got a shoeshine a few years back in the lobby of the Ritz-Carlton in Washington, DC. It was a pretty swanky place. My six-dollar shine was good, but the truth is it just didn't feel the same as when I was a kid at that little barber shop in my hometown. Things change. I get that. But I'd go back if I could, just for a minute or two. It would be great to sit in that big chair again and watch a real expert at work.

The Worst Haircut I Ever Got

by Evans Humphreys

The worst haircut I ever had was when I was ten years old. My hair was very long, and my mom was sick of it. My mom told me we were going to get a video game, but we were actually going to get a haircut.

When we got to the barber shop, the short lady who was to cut my hair told my mother that she didn't speak very good English. So when my mom told her to cut off an inch, she seemed to understand and she said, "Yes … okay."

My mom and my sister left me there alone with the short lady. During the haircut, she showed me how it looked. I was thinking in my head, "This is the worst haircut in the world; I'm going to be laughed at. It's too short!! WAY TOO SHORT!" For the first time in my life I realized I had huge ears. I didn't want to be rude so I said, "This looks great."

When my mom and sister got back, they both said my hair looked fine, because they had to be supportive. I could see in their faces something was wrong. It turns out instead of cutting off an inch, the short lady left an inch.

While we were leaving, the short lady who cut my hair said in broken English, "Too short," with a big smile. That was an understatement!

Early Hair

by Gary Pelton

I grew up with a crewcut, compliments of my dad and his shears. The brothers three would line up on the porch many a Saturday night and, while watching Hockey Night in Canada, get a trim in preparation for church the next day. We each had combs that you slid over your middle finger and brushed your crewcut back. This was an early version of "cool." But, before long it was the seventies and we were letting our hair grow and barbering of most any kind was largely out of the question.

One summer, I worked on a construction crew pouring new sidewalks all around the Detroit area. My hair was a total hassle; in my face, dripping with sweat, and needing constant tending even with a hat or a do-rag. How to keep my long hair and survive work without uncool equipment like a headband? (Believe it or not, I did have to use bobby pins and a hairnet during the fall in the MSU Spartan Marching Band.)

The answer ended up being really quite simple, or so I thought. This was the early 70s and I lived in a hot bed of soul music and fashion, which of course included monster "fros." I would get my hair permed! At best, I would have a sort of white boy fro; at worst it would end up being long curly hair that I could pull back into a pony tail, like long dreads. I floated the idea out there among my buddies and got nothing but peculiar looks and comments, but I was set.

Trip one to the beauty salon and more strange looks and an explanation of a process that would be daunting. I soldiered on (and on and on). Brutal! Small curlers, chemicals, and stuff I don't even remember. But I made it and was soon sporting a pretty cool look; that is, for about a week. Soon it was clear that the perm was not "taking" on the top of my head, so it was back to the beauty shop for a re-do of the do. More curlers, more chemicals, and more strange looks, but again I survived it and soon was back on the street looking good.

And it really was pretty cool for a while. At least that's what I have told myself, photo evidence to the contrary. It seemed to be working on the job and I liked the hip different style I was wearing when I was out. Unfortunately, within a few weeks it happened again: the slow relaxation of the hair on the top of my poor tired scalp. There was no going back to that chamber of hair horrors. So my new plan was to let the hair grow out a while. Surely, the rest of my head would relax, too, and I would naturally be at Plan B in which I would have long curly hair hanging down my head making the regular hair on top look fine.

Didn't happen … What did happen was a nightmare. The hair on the side of my head continued to grow out, but it stayed in stupid little curls. Meanwhile, the hair on the top of my head continued to grow and stretch out like it was meant to do. The result was a look I can only describe as akin to Bozo the Clown sans the shocking red hair color. You remember Bozo. He of the 60s and 70s with the striking red hair horns on the sides of his head with a bald top. Really quite horrifying to think of it now. Well that was me for a shining moment in my young life. If you don't believe me, check out my college ID in 1975.

Within days of that college photo, there was only one thing to do … crewcut!

The Haircut I Never Got

by Ken Wilson

The first haircut I remember getting was at home in suburban Chicago. I must have been six or seven, and my stepmother had me in a chair in the kitchen. I think she was using scissors, but then those were the days when crew cuts were popular, so did she have an electric razor? All I remember clearly is that it didn't go right. "Stay right here," she said, in a worried voice. "I'll be right back." And she left the house. Left and came back a few minutes later with the man next door—the father of a couple of my friends (one of them the boy who one night decided that he himself, his kid brother, and the kid across the street, and I should be the Beatles, and assigned me to be George, the one with the frown I interpreted as a possible sign of meanness). My father was away on a business trip, so in her ... panic? ...who knows ... she went and got that man next door, and when she came back with him they had a consultation. I think she'd managed to cut a sort of hole in the hair at the back of my head—made me prematurely bald before second grade. I do remember that the haircut ended up being more drastic than she'd planned. Maybe a scissor cut turned into a crew cut, I don't know. In any case, the trauma was all hers. Whatever she'd made me look like, I didn't mind. I probably didn't have sense enough to mind.

Nowadays, my wife minds. She approves or disapproves, naturally, of what's been done to my head, because she has to look at it. I still don't care all that much, at least after the second look in the mirror, but I get kindly worded instructions sometimes, which I'm supposed to pass along to the next barber. Something about how the back should be cut. Tapered or not tapered—I'll have to ask her again, I've only been married since '92. My own instructions, after combing what's left of my once blond locks back, not straight across, begin and end with, "Keep it just touching the ears."

My wife remembers what an intriguingly masculine world the barber shop was when her father took her there once, when she was a little girl in Newport News. The swivel chair. The kindly, grey-haired barber who teased her, who sat her on a board he'd put over the arms of the chair to get her head up high enough to work on. He cut her bangs, and her mother, back home when the excursion was over, was not pleased. But my wife had had a big day, a peek into Daddy's world. A peek into the world of men.

Between the sports and hunting magazines, the football calendars, and the occasional *Playboy*, a barber shop always strikes me as a pretty macho world. I have that side of my own personality, but it's something few people would notice, probably, and certainly not barbers, who although or maybe because they do what might in one light be considered somewhat feminine work, washing and grooming male heads, often come across as "He men" with scissors, guys who might not be able to pull railroad trains with their teeth like Charles Atlas, but would sure have fun trying.

So barber's visits are my time to talk sports. I'm only a very casual fan these days, but I draw on deep reservoirs of boyhood enthusiasm for pro football, in particular for the Green Bay Packers. "How is the Pack doing this year?" I ask, especially if I think the guy's old enough to remember the Bart Starr/Vince Lombardi years that climaxed, if not quite culminated, in what's since been dubbed the Ice Bowl. "Can they make the playoffs?" Even though sports are far down my list of interests and identity markers nowadays, and even though my ignorant questions mark me as someone who is *not* up on the really vital stuff in the male world, there is still a sort of elemental male bonding pull I feel when talking sports. And as out of it as I am, I always like hearing the guy, or maybe the guy in the next chair over, talking about his team. I always like saying something/anything that makes me sound, to myself if not to the barber, like a regular Joe. And then I like leaving.

The only remotely upscale, non-sports centered place I've ever gone for a haircut is in the shopping court down below the Watergate Hotel, next door to the Kennedy Center, where my wife and I go several times a year, usually for ballet. The friendly barber I had was pretty suave, or maybe I just saw him that way, him working next door to ... *the Kennedy Center*! I looked not one hair closer to elegant when I left. I was no more coordinated than before. But I felt just the slightest bit ... suave maybe? It was ridiculous, and I knew it was ridiculous, but I indulged it anyhow, just for laughs.

But as much as I enjoyed that experience, like I said, for me one haircut is pretty much as good as another. Only one really stands out—the one I never got. It was in Staunton last summer. I was over there mid-day to hear some free chamber music, and as I walked back to my car afterwards, I passed a barber shop. As soon as I opened the door, I saw it was an African-American shop. And I didn't know what to do. As happily integrated as even the South has become in many day-to-day respects, who has ever seen a black guy in a white barbershop? Or a white guy do what I'd just done, walk into a black shop? Not me. I think the barber and his few customers were as surprised as I was. I sort of stood in the doorway and mumbled something about being from Charlottesville, and he said, politely but a little awkwardly, that he could cut my hair, but that I'd have awhile to wait. And I, I hope politely but perhaps awkwardly, thanked him but told him I didn't have that much time. Had I made a social/racial faux pas? Or did I make one when I left? Would the guy have given me a good haircut? (See above). Did he believe me when I said I didn't have that long to wait? I really did need to get back to Charlottesville. But now … now I really wish I'd stayed.

Barber Shop Memories

by Jim Barns

My first barber shop memory was in 1954 in Towson, Maryland. Along with dogs, baseball was my first love. The Baltimore Orioles had arrived in that year. I remember nothing else about that barber shop except seeing a smiling, amiable guy named Billy Hunter sitting in a chair. Shortstop Billy had come to the Orioles from the Yankees. I followed that smiling face throughout his career. Eventually he became a coach and then manager of the Orioles. I could not help but think that the easy going personality I saw in that barber shop carried him there.

In that period I remember a trip with my mother to a barber shop. While certainly a devoted and loving parent, my mother, a violinist, was a bit of a dreamy sort. A lot was overlooked. Assuming that an eight-year-old would be taking care of personal hygiene would be an example. I was getting my hair cut and the barber called her over. He had practically ruined his scissors while engaged with the dirt in my hair. She was taken aback and bemusedly mentioned this episode over the years. I never got the sense that she realized her neglect. Eventually I came around to a hygiene regimen.

In Charlottesville, there is a storied, good old boys barber shop. I went to it for a while and lucked out with a genial guy. I looked forward to my time with him. I learned that he worked 8–6, six days a week and after working there over 20 years, got one week of vacation. The owner I did not care for, vastly overrated, as confirmed by his treatment of a terrific employee. I righteously stopped going there.

I have had a rogues' gallery of bad haircuts. From the above shop, I went to what was known as "barbers in a box," a small brick building. A female had been hired. Figuring that women are more sensitive, aesthetic, etc., I had hope. I spelled out my history and what I wanted. She scalped me.

For much of my 28 years of marriage, my wife has cut my hair. She does it quickly and rarely have I had a bad haircut. Hundreds of dollars saved and aggravation avoided. I could discard the standard, "Well, it will grow back."

Le Coupe de Cheveux

by Bill Dunnington

It started out as a perfectly fine summer day in Montreal. June 17, 1961, a Saturday, broke clear and sunny, with high wispy white clouds, and a light breeze—perfect for baseball in the park across from our house. We'd all just finished school for the summer: Barney and Michael Colvey, Jean Pierre, Robbie Milne, David Gold, Torstein and Kikki Jacobsen, Dennis Charest, Tom and John Hopkirk, Louise Arnoff, the neighborhood crowd. We'd been done with street shinny since April and I was really looking forward to the first neighborhood ball game of the summer. But things would take a totally unexpected and embarrassing turn for me, even before the first pitch …

I slid onto the breakfast table bench in our kitchen, poised to wolf down a bowl of cereal on the way out the door. My mitt was next to me, still tied around the ball, like it had been all winter, just as keen to get out of the house as me. I was eleven, skinny, with a serious batch of freckles spread across my face like a map of Ireland, and a wavy mop of reddish blond hair.

"Good morning, Billy. It's a beautiful day. I want you to ride your bike up to the Cote de Liesse shopping center and get a haircut first thing. Your grandparents are arriving today, and you need a haircut. I have lots of errands to do and it's time for you to do this. Dad has some chores you can help him with this afternoon. Here's some money to pay the barber. Go ahead and hop on your bike."

"But Mom, we have a baseball game today, this morning, right now—if I'm late, well, I don't want to be the last one picked."

"You have all summer to play in the park. And tonight, you call tell Nana and Grandpa all about your new adventure taking yourself to get a haircut."

My bike had big thick tires. It was a Schwinn. I was kind of embarrassed because everybody else had British bikes with thin tires that just seemed cooler, faster. I was not excited about riding it past the gang in the park, or having to get my hair cut at all. This was a bum deal, all around. Little did I know …

I pedaled the four blocks as quickly as I could and leaned my bike up against the post outside the barber shop. The moment I opened the door I was stopped in my tracks by an overwhelming wave of apprehension. There were five big chairs, all occupied except the middle one, where a slight older man with a white coat and black greasy hair, thinning at the top, stood waiting. I paused, realizing he was French-speaking … and I, not so much. All eyes were on me—I felt like I was walking a gauntlet. Slowly, reluctantly, I climbed up into the chair, feeling (I suppose) like a lamb about to be sheared.

"Bonjour. Que voulez-vous?"

I was speechless. Above the mirror on the wall in front of me was a long array of pictures of grown men, with a full array of various hairstyles. Long and wavy. Butched. Middle part. Slicked back. Bald as an egg. 'Staches. Beards. Long bushy sideburns. There was even a picture of a guy with one huge thick eyebrow that went all the way clear across his forehead before turning up beyond each eye. A monobrow.

Faced with the choice, but unable to convey it in speech, I pointed to the coolest picture on the wall. Wavy, just over the ears, long in front. Cool. "C'est ça," I ventured, hopefully.

He wrapped me up in a brown cape, fastened it behind my neck, got out his clippers, just as I expected, and soon it was buzzing away and my hair was falling in large clumps around me. I was too short in the seat to see myself in the mirror.

With complete confidence in my choice of cuts (and his barbering expertise), my mind drifted to baseball. I wondered who had been chosen onto what teams. How the new bat was to swing. Who was pitching. What the score might already be. My train of thought was totally derailed when all of a sudden, I realized the barber was holding my head and had begun rubbing a block of hard wax over my head from front to back. Ouch. I don't want this. I stiffened. He squeezed harder. Can't you stop? This is not what I asked for. But I couldn't stop him.

Sure enough, when he finally stopped, I stood up and looked in the mirror, I was shocked to see that I had been totally butched. Seriously flat-topped. Hair waxed up stiff as a board. Not a wave in sight. He took off the cape, I gave him the money and briefly spotted his grin as I bolted out the door.

Onto my bike, pedaling furiously. Home. Nobody can see this. This is awful. The wax stinks. My hair isn't blowing in the wind. Past the park. Please, nobody see me. Into the driveway. Upstairs to the bathroom. Head under the sink faucet. Why won't this wax come out?

Some hours later, rather hungry, I ventured sheepishly out of my room, faced with the prospects of explaining this ultimate misfortune ... who knows how many times ... and wondering how long I would have to endure it.

It's been years since I've seen anyone with such a classic but horrendous haircut. But I've have since learned to say, in English (and French), "Same style, shorter all around, over the ears, I'll get the burns and the brow."

A Tale of Three Barbers

by Michael Kuchinski

My first barber, at least the first one that I have any recollection of, was a man named Frank. His shop was just down the street from our house in Pennsylvania, in a little cluster of stores that included a small market and a florist. Even for his day, Frank was decidedly old school, and notably, not a member of the barber's union. He was open for business on Mondays, whereas union shops were not, but he was closed Saturdays when they were open. As I recall, Frank's haircuts were cheap, even by the standards of the late 50s and early 60s. Being non-union, I suppose, enabled him to undersell the competition.

When I was small, my mother would accompany me to Frank's and give him instructions on how he should cut my hair. But once I got older, and graduated from the booster chair, I ventured there on my own, walking the two or three blocks, carrying just enough money in my pocket to cover the cost of my haircut. Frank always cut my hair short, leaving me with just barely enough to comb. In the summer he would cut it shorter still, buzzing it down to crew cut length.

Frank's shop was a dingy little place. He had only two barber chairs, both of which featured the brand name Hercules. Occasionally, he would have a partner working there with him, but mostly, Frank worked alone. His waiting area consisted of two or three metal-framed chairs, and a table strewn with old issues of *Field and Stream*. After I had paid for my haircut, Frank would give me a piece of Bazooka bubble gum. I did not chew gum, but not wanting to offend Frank, I always accepted it politely.

As I grew older and boys started wearing their hair longer, Frank's haircuts became too unhip. My contemporaries always seemed to be much cooler than me. I remember one classmate in particular who often bragged about his expensive haircuts. He also wore the latest clothes and drove a new sports car. (He subsequently turned out to be a drug dealer.) Since I already felt alienated from my classmates, I didn't want my haircut to make this disaffection even worse. As money was always a consideration in our household, any option had to be within our budget. So, I hit upon a solution that would be virtually cost free. I asked my mother to cut my hair.

Armed with a comb, a pair of barber scissors, and a magazine article entitled "Great Family Haircuts at Home," she agreed. For my last two years of high school and throughout college mom cut my hair. Even when I went away to graduate school, she continued in her role as my barber, cutting my hair when I would come home during the university's semester breaks. But when I took a job in Virginia after graduation, my visits home became more infrequent, as did my haircuts.

Meanwhile, my new girlfriend and soon-to-be wife said my hair was too long. The 70s were over, and she wanted me to affect a more preppy look. In addition to buying me some alligator shirts and khaki pants, she also persuaded me to visit the shop of a man named Fran. Now strictly speaking, Fran was a not a barber, but rather a hair stylist, whose customers included women as well as men. (I remember one particularly awkward visit when my mother-in-law was getting a shampoo, cut, and blow-dry in the chair next to me.) Fran gave me a more contemporary look, and as the years went by did his best to conceal the fact that my hair was rapidly thinning on top. (Male-pattern baldness runs in my family on my mother's side. Both of my mother's brothers were either bald or receding.)

One day I came to Fran with a special request. I had just been diagnosed with non-Hodgkin's lymphoma, and was about to undergo chemotherapy. I knew that I would eventually lose all my hair, and so I asked Fran to cut it very short, so that when my hair did begin to fall out, there would be less of it to lose.

Shortly thereafter, following my first treatments, my hair did indeed begin to fall out. Even worse, it fell out in patches and clumps, so I took my razor and shaved it all off. Throughout the remainder of my treatments, I had no need of a barber. Furthermore, chemo doesn't just affect the hair on your head, but all body hair, even eyebrows and eyelashes. For the first few months of treatment, I managed to maintain a scraggily moustache. Then one morning I awoke to find one side of it had fallen out completely, so I shaved off the remaining side.

Thankfully, after four or five months of treatment my doctor declared that I was in remission. Gradually, my hair began to grow back in, just down-like fuzz at first, but then real hair, at least around the fringes. I was still balding on top, and briefly considered a comb-over, but instead decided to keep the close-cropped look that Fran had given me when I first began treatment. Whatever else you may say about it, it is low maintenance. (Note to all men with thinning hair: Ditch your comb-over! Embrace your baldness, become one with it!)

And so my tonsorial journey has come full circle. My current haircut is not that different from Frank's summertime crew cuts of yore. The only difference now is that a haircut costs more, even though I have less hair to cut!

Little Joe and John's

by Ed Banks

Around the fourth grade I determined that I would never get my hair cut again. However, I had been conscripted into a K–8 Catholic school. I was able to fight off my mother's demands for me to get my hair cut but there was a higher power, the Principal, Sister Teresa-Marie. The school had a rule that boy's hair could not be more than collar length and so every couple months Sister Teresa-Marie would inform my mother that I would face detention unless my hair was cut to their standards. I believe my mother and Sister Teresa-Marie formed an unholy alliance to get my hair cut. I still refused and served detention which was not too bad; I basically had to sit in her office and wrap coins from the Sunday collections.

Time ran out on me and I got dragged to Little Joe and John's Barber Shop. Joe and John were indeed little and they stood on footstools to chop off my hair. This torture went on until eighth grade. My parents made me apply to the two Catholic high schools in the area and I got accepted to both. I told them I was not going to any more Catholic schools because I did not like the rules. The hair cut thing was a big part of it. My mother cried and my father was thrilled (no tuition). I went to the public high school and there are many pictures of me and my unruly hair from those days. Oscar Gamble and Bake McBride have nothin' on me.

I don't know if it happened on the same day as my first enforced haircut, but I used to wear a POW/MIA copper bracelet for Vietnam soldiers. It had the soldier's name on it, the date he went missing, and a serial number. As the USA started bringing the boys home there was a list everyday in the newspaper (you all remember those things, newspapers) of who got home and I would check for "my guy" every day. He finally made it home safe and sound and my mother came into Little Joe and John's Barber Shop to pick me up and informed me that "my guy" had made it back. I was thrilled he was back but disappointed that I didn't see it first because I was being held hostage in the barber's chair. So the protocol was that you took off your bracelet (it snapped in half in the barber's chair) and mailed it to the soldier with a thank you note. He lived somewhere in Nebraska. My wrist stayed green for several days even after I took the copper bracelet off.

The Hand

by Paul Erb

Clotho, Lachesis, Barber. Those are the Three Fates. And at the end, whatever Barber did, is what you publish. The rest is on the floor, and there's no CTL-Z.

It is not going too far to say that once you've sat in the chair, your barber is your editor, your translator. You don't own him; you *rent* him, on his own terms. You bring what has grown out of you, the best you've naturally got. And even though whatever you bring is yours, it's the best you can do, and you're desperate, so you just sit there while he does what he wants with it.

When I was little, our mother cut our hair in the bathroom, to save money. I can still smell the acrid mineral oil that came with the clippers, and which she used to lubricate the buzzing blades. *Chk-vzzzzzzzzzz.* Until about 1968 my brother and I got crew cuts this way, and that's who I was then—curious, diligent, a worshipper of Jerry Kramer, the Green Bay Packers, and the lost JFK.

Then suddenly, after the 1968 Democratic National Convention in Chicago, the whole world started watching. My father started wearing jeans, and any kind of interference with hair became a moral offense. Our hair fell freely into our faces: first into our eyes, so we could toss our heads with defiance (and to see); then over my face; and then, as curls took charge in puberty, in bushy styles that took up a lot of air space.

At 14, in defiance of my family's Frugality Oath, I went to the new hairstylist on the University of Richmond campus. A stylist on a campus was the safest option, legitimated by black-and-white *Life* magazine photographs of defiant university protests opposite poised ads for men with carefully tended hair near smiling girls in tight shirts and miniskirts.

It was a pretty good cut. The family acted indignant and felt compelled to condemn it as *not what we do.*

Meanwhile, my hair continued to assert itself. It grew faster, thicker, stiffer. I was embarrassed that I understood women who said, "I can't do a *thing* with it." When I dragged myself out of bed in the morning, it was a case of unmitigated revolt, a sloppy Rod McKuen mess all over my head pretending to do something. My high-school culture—thank God—was dominated by all things Afro, so I dressed in bellbottom doubleknits or baggy pants, fitting in with hair as big as I could make it and chanting rhythms at pep rallies. But the hair was just pretending to obey. Photographs from the period attest to the unrest on my head. It was awful.

Until I felt The Hand. I don't even remember where this barber shop was, exactly, or how old I was. Somewhere in Richmond, Virginia, in a little barber shop where I stepped in desperately to resolve the mess up top, I landed accidentally in a chair in front of a barber almost certainly 75 years old.

When he put his hand on my head, I felt a power-surge of confident experience. He knew my head! He knew my hair! How was this possible?

It is hard to overestimate the power of this ocean-surge, like being picked up by a beach wave so high that for a moment you can see above the dune and all across the highway to the other side of the road. Suddenly, in a humble barber's chair, when his hand touched my scalp above my right ear, I felt a confidence that the sweep of history had gathered itself into this one moment, *hic et nunc sempiternam.*

I stared into the mirror to see who he was. It was Merlin; it was Gandalf; it was Enkidu; it was Teiresias; it was Confucius; it was an old man. He didn't care about me at all, and didn't pretend to. He was a model of classical mastery, unaffected by fashion or style. He knew heads, and he knew hair. And the comfort of my being one of many, but being received by a hand that instantly knew my head, and gave a clean cut that suited me, was an endorsement of the whole classical world, I was to learn of later, an attitude to work that suits mankind in the longer run.

I went back months later for a repeat, and learned that the magician had passed away. I sat down in another's chair. The Hand was not at all the same.

I have not seen nor trusted any other barber since, and have never come across a hand I trusted more. But the classical world persists, and the quest for The Hand continues.

Staples Barber Shop and the Carrs

by David Wilkinson Carr, Jr.

Staples Barber Shop, run by the senior Mr. Staples, has been in the Barracks Road Shopping Center in Charlottesville since the 1950s. Carrs have been in Albemarle County since the 1730s. My great- great grandfather, George Carr was born in 1800, and knew Jefferson and Lafayette. (He helped settle Jefferson's estate as a young lawyer.) George's grandson, George (son of David), born in 1893, frequented Staples' shop in the 50s and 60s. At the same time, his son, David W. Carr (1924) had his ears lowered by the proprietor. As a young boy in the 60s my curly blond locks were also shorn by Mr. Staples. At times, my father, David, or grandfather, George, would take me with them to the shop, but it was usually my mom taking my brother, George, and me. And of course, when my son Wilkinson Micajah Carr returned to Charlottesville from his Seattle birthplace when he was one, his father and grandfather quickly introduced him to the senior Mr. Staples and his scissors.

Staples became an institution and my 90-year-old dad still gets his hair cut there. Mr. Staples, senior, has since passed on, but we were pleased to have him cut the hair of four generations of Carrs.

SWIPES

by Tony Zentgraf

Vietnam and racial issues were heating up in the summer of 1965, but it was an innocent time for an eleven-year-old in Baltimore. My duties included parochial school and Sunday Mass with an occasional trip to the doctor or dentist. The remaining hours were filled with my friends Charles and Andrew playing every sport we knew and whatever game we could create. The city was under stress and the country ready to erupt, but the O's were one year away from a World Championship and the Colts were expected to win again. We had our own tensions caused by a simple trip to the barber. Crew cuts were in and sometimes we got a flat top that was finished off with Butch Wax and the usual Jeris. Saturday at the barber was equal in misery to two holy days in a row requiring High Mass. One of the outcomes, other than itching and neck irritation, was that it was clear to all that you had visited the barber. The agony in the chair was nothing compared to the next twenty four hours back in the neighborhood where you were open game for what we called swipes.

On your shiny new neck, friends or family could give you swipes. Using their thumb, they started at the base of your neck, and quickly slid the thumb toward your ear saying, "I got swipes." The act would cause extreme pain similar to a rope burn. For some reason, swipes could only be administered once within the twenty four hours following your haircut. If someone attempted a second try, the recipient of swipes was obliged to punch the law breaker in the nose.

You would never swipe anyone you didn't know because it was a familial, communal practice. It was always more dangerous to swipe your brother because retaliation was certain—anger genes and Catholicism were too powerful to overcome. Strong friendships were built when swipes resulted in a fight.

Neighborhood boys had to wear the all-white first communion suit, serve six a.m. Mass, put on coat and tie for school, and give and receive swipes gracefully. Swipes were expected, short lived, and forgivable. If you resisted at all, you were held down and swiped by younger brothers which could be humiliating. So it was better to accept swipes willingly, then seek revenge accordingly.

We pitched Double Bubble baseball cards, just like we pitched pennies. If you were closest to the wall, you won—and could possibly collect a Micky Mantle or a Willie Mays. I was about to throw an Al Kaline—a south Baltimore native and a hall of fame Detroit Tiger. At the exact moment of release, Jerome issued a fair swipes. I lost Kaline and illegally punched Jerome in the chest. We had a long altercation across several properties and in the end I socked him in the nose and knocked his glasses to the ground. Fortunately his glasses were not broken, but that blow finished the fight. Jerome ran inside from embarrassment, I was the victor, but had no stomach for celebration because I knew I was a jerk. I contested the swipe because I was so mad about the loss of Al Kaline. I had no case since Jerome's swipe was within the twenty-four-hour clause. Because I was raised Catholic, I felt a great deal of guilt over the fight and even cried about it because Jerome, like Charles and Andrew, was a good buddy. So we shook hands and went on.

The barber shop itself was an intimidating place because you were among men who had been at D-Day, the 38th parallel, or Saigon. You did not speak unless spoken to and if you acted childish, the response was a look that caused nightmares. So you shut up, sucked it up, and pretended that the cut was just another ho-hum moment in your life. If you were an athlete and they knew it, they gave you the respect of a Private First Class—but that was all. If you opened your mouth at the wrong time, you could be court-martialed.

Barbershop Saturday ruined a lot of weekends because with Mass on Sunday, you got no break—and with the potential for swipes, life was made all the worse. In the 1960s a unique thing happened in the Catholic Church: Saturday evening Mass was created. So, you could take all your lumps in one day, and if you got a haircut early enough on Saturday, swipes would be over by the time you slept in a little on Sunday. Thank God for Vatican II.

The anxiety of the barber shop has mostly subsided over the last fifty years. I have sat in many different chairs since and really enjoyed some relaxing minutes. I do not talk nor do I want to, conversations go on, and I barely listen. The sound of the clippers almost puts me to sleep and I could spend a longer time there than required if they would let me. There is no rush to get down, no veterans sneering at a little punk, no fear of swipes.

But, if some wise guy from Baltimore were to run into me post haircut and yell, "I got swipes," my stomach would turn, heart rate would increase—my fight or flight response. Even though giving in was the most practical option to accept your swipes, it was Harry Reimers who one time avoided swipes for the regulation twenty four hours. He was bruised and battered from jumping over fences, hiding in sewer lines, and climbing up fire escapes. We never caught him and so from that moment on Reimers was a neighborhood hero. We didn't know it at the time, but we were going to need a lot of heroes before the end of the sixties.

The *Trimmer Comb* and Other Tales

by Dave Krovetz

I was five years old in 1961 when my family—mom, dad, two boys, and one girl—moved from the Twin Cities to central Florida. Although I have many memories of my early years in Minnesota, I have no recollection of haircuts from that time. None-the-less, photos from those days confirm that my hair was short, very short. And that can only mean one thing— my barber was my mother.

Mom was always a one-length-fits-all type of barber. She'd march us boys into the kitchen where we'd sit in turn on a tall, fire engine red, two-step kitchen stool. There was never any question about length or style; this was the 60s and we were going to have conservative, short, and practical haircuts. Mom would proceed to buzz-cut each of us in turn. Perhaps my sister was accorded the luxury of professional hairstyling, but for us boys, it was always wash and wear, no maintenance hair, the Beatles be damned.

At the time I entered junior high school we were living in rural Maryland, an hour outside of Baltimore. Teenage boys—or at least yours truly at 13—really did not want their mom cutting their hair. After a trip to the local barber was less than successful, mom upped the ante on the home-haircut game: I was given a *Trimmer Comb*.

The *Trimmer Comb* was a quintessential 70s device: clamshell-shaped, it fit in the palm of one's hand. The leading edge of a *Trimmer Comb* held a pair of straightedge razor blades hidden behind comb-like teeth, while the trailing edge used a single blade similarly placed behind teeth of a shorter length. The devilishness of the *Trimmer Comb* lay in the details (and results) of its use. Using my *Trimmer Comb* necessitated facing the bathroom mirror for guidance as I performed successive sweeps with the comb across my scalp. If—as in my case—a person has the least inclination towards dyslexia, then cutting one's hair guided by a mirror's reflection is a surefire way to accentuate the problem. A few top-of-the-head passes with the comb, then a touch-up trim on the left—or is that the right?—a second pass to correct an overcorrection; this process only ended once my hair was again short-cropped and unstylish. In theory, I was in charge of my haircutting and thus had no one else to blame for this mess but myself. Score one point in Mom's quest for keeping things short and practical.

By the mid-70s I'd matriculated at the University of Virginia, newly coed and located in sleepy but growing Charlottesville, Virginia. As a *First Year*—never a freshman at the University—I lived in the "old dorms," specifically in Emmet. The *old dorms* were never to be confused with the *new dorms* located around the corner by the stadium. The *new dorms* were modern suites, while the *old dorms* consisted of long halls of traditional double rooms, one hall stacked above another. Emmet's lower two floors housed men, while the uppermost floor housed women. No air-conditioning, no Internet, and a payphone at the end of the hall. We bunked two to a room that measured 12 by 16 feet.

The guys on my hall were an eclectic mix: Bubba—drafted out of high school by the Orioles as a pitcher—could hit a bulls-eye on the payphone dial with a tennis ball; Bostonian George, who regaled us with tales of summer sailing on the family yacht; and Tony, hailing from New Jersey, whose dad was a first generation Italian-immigrant and a barber. Upon graduating high school, Tony had to choose between barbering school and life as a Wahoo, opting for the latter in pursuit of a Liberal Arts education. Tony's conversation was filled with stories of the lore and precision of true barbering. He could shave a balloon covered in shaving cream without popping it. He could cut hair (and brought his personal set of professional barbering scissors to school). He was a born entrepreneur. On Friday afternoons, Tony would set up a chair in the hallway outside of his room and cut hair at five dollars a head. Always good for a decent haircut, Tony never lacked for customers.

Post University, I discovered Oak Hill Barbering and Styling in the countryside south of Charlottesville. Situated alongside a run-down trailer park and next door to a country store, Oak Hill Barbering and Styling was housed in a small cinderblock and wood building. Oak Hill Barbering and Styling was a one-man shop, owned and operated by Jim Shank. Jim—on the short side, bald as a bowling ball, and decidedly rotund—exuded warmth and personality. I never figured out the Styling aspect of Oak Hill Barbering and Styling, Jim was a barber through and through.

Jim's shop was the same size and just as cozy and cluttered as my dorm room in Emmet. Upon entering the shop, one found a dozen chairs for waiting customers scattered along three walls. Because selling pocketknives formed a lucrative sideline, Jim's pocketknife collection filled two walls of shelving. A glass-topped display case that presented an array of combs, brushes, and salves filled out the third wall, while the shop's lone barbering chair—along with the tools of the barbering trade—filled the fourth and final wall. In that chair sat one customer, while Jim cut hair, answered the phone, and held forth to one and all, this occasionally interrupted by men dropping by to talk knives or make a purchase. Jim's conversation contained equal parts of local gossip, barbershop humor, and community news. His conversational fodder was gleaned from his clientele: University professors, students, and blue-collar workers of Charlottesville. Jim's knowledge of local lore and gossip was encyclopedic. One left Oak Hill Barbering and Styling with less hair on the scalp, but a bit more beneath it.

As the years roll by, I seem to need less hair cut with each haircut. I've slowly drifted back to cutting my own hair. In that sense, I suppose I'm back to square one. I cut my hair standing in front of the bathroom mirror, my reflection for guidance, using an old Wahl electric clipper, now on its second or third set of blades. I cut my hair as short as possible, striving for a practical, wash and wear, no maintenance, definitely no styling type of trim.

A Greenwich Village Barber Shop

by Sam Carr

I was eager about my trip to the barber. On a holiday, I wanted to immerse myself in the melting pot culture that is lower Manhattan. It was Friday after Thanksgiving, and I was bivouacking with my Southern emigre brother-turned Wall Street banker, who had quarters in artsy Greenwich Village not far from Union Square. The markets being open for a few hours that day, he had to "go into the office" before we were to rendezvous at the Neue Galerie. So I had to entertain myself on this dreary day in the City. The famed department stores and Rockefeller Center had to be avoided at all costs, on this Black Friday, and it was too cold for much of a walking tour. And my invitations to lunch at 21 or the University Club must have been misplaced.

"Go to Frank's. It's an Italian place—they are actually 'off the boat' Italian. But they've been here a while. Nice guys. Joe and Sal are good. Frank is good too, but he's old." John instructed me in his calm, measured, but authoritative banker's voice. "It's just south of Washington Square, on Thompson Street. Walk down Fifth Avenue and keep going through the Square. If you see Frank, tell him John sent you and says, 'Hi.'"

After some meandering around the arch in Washington Square, I found the cubbyhole of a shop. Around the three old-time chairs squeezed in the small room, two older Italian men shuffled while attending to a customer and a third folded towels. From the gritty street I stepped into the warm shop, and obeying the pointing motion from the near Italian man who paused folding towels and gestured me to sit, I eased into the middle chair. The chair embraced me like the one at the dentist office, and though comfortable, I tensed at the prospect of a haircut from a stranger.

As a Scots-Irish Southern boy, personal independence has encouraged me to handle my own grooming, laundry, shoe shining, and other affairs to the extent possible. And if I did outsource work, as a young man I did so to another member of my clan as much as possible. And as the grandson of people who came of age during the Great Depression—my grandfather went to a CCC camp as a young man for work—I justified my behavior in economic terms. As Frank draped the apron over me, I was second-guessing my indulgence in this Big City haircut when I knew well I could either trim it myself or hire barber services back below the Mason-Dixon line where goods and services are generally cheaper. Any reservations that might have been arising in the back of my mind were dispelled when I recognized the Italian music had given way to the soothing vocals of Dean Martin. The music hit me, and my muscles relaxed and I sunk into the chair.

"How do you want your hair?" Frank asked with the professionalism of a waiter at a fine restaurant taking an order.

"Ah, I suppose just a regular trim. Maybe a little shorter on the sides and back."

Frank replied with a slight bow of the head and a mild grunt to indicate that he understood, and proceeded to step into his work with the gaiety of a street musician stepping into a solo.

"By the way, my brother John sent me here—short dark brown hair, from Memphis, John."

"Ah yes, John. Nice young man. He brings his girlfriend here too. You know, she has short hair, so we trim it for her. It looks real nice! Those salons, it's not fair what they charge the girls."

"Ha, yes. I know. It does look good."

Frank was shearing away at my dirty blond hair which sprinkled onto my smock and the floor. Joe and Sal, I presumed, were busy dancing around the other customer, while the door behind me opened and shut several times as a delivery man dropped off packages of supplies. With a little small talk and holiday cheer—I think the delivery man had had some holiday "spirits"—the little shop buzzed like the rhythm of a jazz song. This lasted until the delivery man overstayed his welcome, and for a moment there was some tension from Frank that the delivery man didn't pick up. The delivery man was interrupting the song of these men working. And the shop was too small for the delivery man to be much more than a momentary fixture. With a glare from Frank, the deliveryman was dismissed.

I was transfixed on my image in the mirror and in the periphery taking in the images of Frank and his colleagues moving around the shop. As I cautiously surveyed progress, I began to rather enjoy myself.

"How's this?" Frank asked gesturing to the back, holding a hand mirror to the side to better emphasize the back.

"Ah, yes. Could you shape it a bit more?"

Frank nodded politely and resumed. He progressed with some more rapid snipping against the teeth of the comb he was using to lift the hair.

"Could you give me a shave, too?"

Frank nodded and looked toward Sal. The way middle infielders communicate around second base with looks and subtle signals, Sal got the signal and stepped over to contraptions to heat some towels and shaving cream. I got the sense that not many patrons requested this service. But I thought I would treat myself to the "works."

Frank tipped my chair back, and I felt like taking a nap. He covered my face with warm towels, while I could hear him prep his straight razor against the strop. As I was nearly horizontal with him standing over me, he removed the towels, and with this blade against my throat, I was completely in his hands as if he were my surgeon and I was on a gurney and he were preparing to operate. Only in this case, I wasn't anesthetized. As he worked on my face, I felt the steadiness of his hand, and rather than being skeptical of his wrinkles, I viewed his signs of aging as a badge of sorts. A straight razor in someone else's hands could be a weapon, but for Frank, it was his brush or his chisel.

Frank gently palmed my forehead and tilted my head from side to side, and methodically shaved away. After every stroke, however long or short, he wiped the blade on the towel draped over his left arm. Few young bucks have the stomach to whip a blade around human features the way his old timer could. Nor would they have the touch with the classic shaving implements. The fact that he was Italian was comforting given his home country's reputation for producing men artful with their hands. The novelty of this experience encouraged me to grin, but I held back lest I grin too much and lose some flesh. Twice he retouched the generous shaving cream beard that made me resemble Santa Claus.

When Frank pulled my nose from side to side, then up, I knew that the shave was nearly concluded. He then took a few more warm towels and placed them around my face. While he readied a bowl of water and some aftershave lotion, the warm towels seemed to steam my freshly naked face. When Frank pulled the towels off, I looked down in shock at the white cotton with droplets of my red blood. He got me, I thought. Frank looked cautious and waited for my reaction, but I assured him that I just had sensitive skin which was true.

After a firm handshake with the proprietor and a few waves to the other attendants, I paid my bill and left a handsome tip as I was replaced in the chair with another mane to be cropped. I stepped out into Washington

Square for a new adventure, where the wind cut even more unencumbered against my face and the remnants of the mop on my head, now a sharp new hairdo, blew in the wintery gust. Frank was the last person I let give me a shave. I save that for special occasions.

The Reincarnation of Mahatma Gandhi

by Neal H. Gropen

A lot of life is predetermined for us.
Either by our times.
Our culture
or by small details like …

Units of measure. Who the hell ever put twelve inches on one foot?
Or made fifteen sixteenths less than thirty one thirty seconds?

Me. I think the shape of the state you live in makes a big difference. At the end of high school in the summer, I got caught down in the left hand ragged end of the state of Virginia. This state's shape they say is a function of the mountainous terrain. But my first visit to Wise, Virginia, during that summer proved to me that elevated humidity simply had wrinkled the cartographer's paper. And, that our Old Dominion might have been pristinely rectangular were it not for that overpowering element, water.

It may have been a reward for something scholastic or an honor to suffer quietly. But, a number of us got scholarships. Were quarantined. Aided and abetted the conservation movement. And learned about ecology, the natural world, and if bears lift the seat when they use the toilet.

The humidity in Wise County combined with the boredom of dormitory life added up and became too much for this one juvenile. I don't know what got into me, but the thought of cutting hair was involved, as it was hot. Hair insulates and curly hair insulates better.

So I waited till everyone went to the cafeteria. It must have been premeditated. I don't know. I got a razor and started removing my hair; scissors would have better to take away the bulk of it, but I didn't really plan on taking all of it off. Was I thinking of a Mohawk, or some foolish expression of individuality. Who knows what lurks in the mind?

Eventually I shaved the scalp and got to fresh skin. It was a cooling, smooth, ball bearing like feeling. There is nothing else much like it. Ask any of us bald guys. The closest thing to a bald head is your knee. Hair provides a cushion (from impact, abrasion, radiation, and heat loss).

Well my old eighteen-year-old silly self decided to be just that. Silly. And bald.

I covered myself with a white bed sheet. Sat at the top of the stairs. Wrapped and seated à la Mahatma Gandhi contemplating the four human elements—love, hate, fear, and cooperation.

Snow's

by Bob Kusyk

Second grade isn't supposed to be traumatic. In fact it wasn't for me either, but all the same, it sure didn't start out with a bang. This was going to be a difficult year for the Browns, as at the onset of summer training camp, the incomparable Jim Brown decided to concentrate full time on climbing a new mountain. After leading Cleveland to the past two NFL Title games (winning one of them 27–0 in the icy December mud), the great #32 telegrammed from the London set of *The Dirty Dozen* that it was go-time for a new challenge. Becoming a major Hollywood leading man meant that his days wearing shoulder pads and an orange helmet were over.

As a responsible fan, this required even more focus to ease the Browns into the next season, and listening to the final pre-season game in my lucky upstairs position next to a brother's radio, I vowed that if we couldn't score on this particular third quarter drive, dramatic action would be necessary. After all, these exhibitions were important at setting the tone of championship-caliber efforts. Thus, a seemingly simple square-out that was thrown beyond the reach of Paul Warfield put Plan B into action— as I marched into the other bedroom, grabbed the scissors, and felt the gratifying sensation of three decisive snips—and then followed the orders coming from downstairs to "turn that damn radio off and go to bed."

Sunday morning meant the long drive to the weird gathering my mother belonged to, and as she took one look at me before going to the car, she screamed "What happened to your hair? We can't take you inside a church looking like that!" I'll grant you that perhaps my cut wasn't a prize-winner, but it turned the neat trick of postponing yet another fire-and-brimstone lecture on the evils of coffee and beer. Moreover, to those in the know, it would be seen as critical to team success when the season's inspirational stories were re-told as the corks popped in late December.

So far, so good—and I'd take my chances on the school playground that my square-outs would be on the money at the first recess Monday. It was looking like blue skies for me, though I'd have to practice a few tosses wearing a baseball cap to be certain I was ready—and I was, only nicking the house a few times while otherwise whistling the ball above and through the porch opening. But alas, the absurd lineup for picture-day was on the school docket, and instead of dropping back and zipping a spiral to my right before "three alligator" unleashed the pass rush, I was escorted to Snow's Barber Shop before the flashbulb could officially chronicle my surgery.

Snow's was chosen for the simple reason that it was the first of its species to open on Mondays. It was to be my maiden voyage to its humble shores. Across Solon Road and stuffed between the K of C Hall and the Dog Pound, this modest brick building wasn't built for charm school— Mr. Snow was serious and intent while listening to my mother's tale of parental woe. All I could hear was the shlacking of his razor increase on that beefy belt when he was told that "something must have got into him on Saturday night." Indeed something did—4th and 8 situations on our own 35 were no less tolerable then as now. But old Mr. Snow was up to the challenge, promising to "even things up" no matter what was about to appear when the red hat with the blue C was removed.

Told that I now "looked like a man instead of one of those damned Beatles," I was asked by Mr. Snow to reflect on his cut as the artiste handed me his mirror. I bit my lower lip—hard—and vowed to not remove a now surprisingly loose baseball cap until 3rd grade.

However, when the second-oldest brother returned home from his first college break, it was time for a trip back to Snow's before Christmas, as getting across Solon Road by myself was not yet in the cards. And I was a-ok with the notion of making something better out of the brown mop that half-heartedly emerged through a disappointing second place season. Wearing a red baseball cap on Thanksgiving night watching the year go down the tubes in the Cotton Bowl, home of the Dallas Cowboys, just wasn't the top of the food chain.

So on a windy, flurried December, I crossed Solon Road again. This time the visit was in the graying afternoon and instead of hearing only Snow's shoes on the tile with the snips and whirs of his machinery, I was treated to a conversation of the adult male variety. Brother was also sized up. After all, he was of the notional age of a Beach Boy and his look was decidedly not that of a kid on his way to Vietnam. However, he declined the chance to have his next semester's opportunity for meeting a girl from the west coast shorn away, and as it were, I was sent to the proverbial chair.

The rematch with Mr. Snow was heavy with the possibility that it would go the way of the first bout, of which the outcome was pre-ordained. I analyzed the current situation—and when I later learned the word "gulag" I knew the place where they could have taken the Polaroid. Snow didn't see a problem with keeping his shop on the cool side—and anyway, who's going to complain to a guy with a trembling hand when he's got a pair of scissors and your back is to him? But something odd happened at the instant Snow was about to dig in for the main course … a crony of his burst in the door and yelled out, "Didja hear, Walt Disney just died … and he wanted them to freeze his body!" Old Snow dropped his scissors and I started to cry.

I got out of that chair and the barber shop before Snow, or my brother, could stop me. "What got into that kid?" All I knew was the one person who could make me laugh on Sunday nights was gone. And when I started running across Solon Road, I knew they could have done Walt's bidding by throwing him into the empty chair next to mine. December in that place was colder than, I guess, the other side of Pluto.

Two Vignettes

by Jim Donahue

Barber or Dentist???

As a young lad who adored sweets, especially candy, and being before the fluoridation of water, I had more than my fair share of cavities and trips to the dentist. Perhaps if I had paid a little more attention to dental hygiene I would have been much better off. Monthly trips to the dentist's office were common and Novocain, administered with fearfully long needles, and laughing gas, were common anesthetics used in the 1940s.

Haircuts were also a monthly adventure and I had to sit in those confounded "booster" seats. How humiliating!! I wanted to be older so that I could sit unassisted in the barber chair like the big boys did.

Whenever my dad brought me to the barber, upon entering the room, I vividly recall becoming frightened, as I wasn't sure if I was at the dentist office or at the barbershop. I was immediately relieved when I recognized the barber, our neighbor, Mr. Gorman. He was such a kind man in comparison to that mean old dentist, Dr. Sadow. The movie "Little Shop of Horrors" brought back vivid memories of my visits to the dentist.

A Spiteful Confederate Barber

My mom and dad moved from Massachusetts to Culpeper, Virginia after he retired in 1977. Being a Yankee his entire life he wasn't sure what to expect from the southern gentry.

Shortly after moving in to his new home he went to visit the local barber. Not recognizing my dad, the barber asked where he was from. My dad, with his very pronounced "Brahmin" accent, told him that he was from Framingham, Massachusetts.

The barber looked over my dad's head of hair and announced, "So you're a damn Yankee." My dad thought that he was just kidding but the barber proceeded to use his shears to cut my dad's hair very close to the scalp. My dad told me it went something like this:

"Here's for General Robert E. Lee," with a sweeping motion front to back on the left side of his head. "And here's to General Stonewall Jackson," as he applied the shears to the right side of his head. And finally over the top the shears ran and the barber announced "And this is for General Jubal Early."

When my dad returned home my mom exclaimed with horror, "What barber did you go to?" as he was virtually scalped. Needless to say my dad never returned to that barber shop and I think that my mom became his regular barber thereafter.

First Haircut

by Corky Schoonover

It was an exquisite sunny spring Saturday, the kind of day that puts a bounce in your step, a smile on your face, and energizes you for the tasks at hand. I had a big one that day that involved my older son, then five years-old: his first haircut at a barber shop. While maybe not on the magnitude of his first words or first steps, it was still an important ritual that would incrementally move him along the path from boy to man and further forge the bond between a father and son. *And*, I was in charge of making it happen.

My wife had been cutting his hair up to that point and I must commend her on the job she'd done: bowl cut, no part, trimmed evenly all the way around and very cute. We agreed though, that it was time for the next step. It seemed logical to go to the shop that I had been frequenting since we'd moved downtown nearly a decade earlier. An unassuming one-story rectangular brick building, it was located on a busy corner; surrounded by a thriving restaurant on the third side and a venerable accounting firm on the fourth, I surmised that developers had been salivating over the spot for years.

The owner and proprietor, Ed Shifflett, had no intention of selling, though; at 61 he was still spry though slightly hunched over even then. He was an avid walker and golfer in his down time and commanded chair #1 as you entered the front door. At chair #2 was Wilbert, trim and round faced, wire rim glasses, hair carefully parted and slicked back. Like Ed he liked to chat but unlike Ed, who stayed totally on task, Wilbert would sometimes pause to emphasize in his gentlemanly Virginia accent an important point about his passion away from work, gardening, while using his scissors to gesture. Roy, older and stationed at #3 was tall, very quiet, and almost impossibly thin with a gaunt face, but was a fine barber and soon to retire as it turned out. Finally, Forest, the youngest, worked chair #4. Short and stocky with a big bushy brown mustache, his most notable trait was that he talked more slowly than anyone I'd ever been around. Fortunately, his hair cutting did not follow suit.

I confidently brought my son to this group; what could go wrong? I'd had consistently good haircuts from each of the four and now I could proudly introduce my son to the ambience of their shop and barber shops in general. I wondered what he would notice first. Would it be the piles of hair on the floor and him wondering who they came from? Would it be the TV mounted, curiously, on a platform above the waiting customers, facing the barber chairs, so that they couldn't actually see it? As a result it provided a background drone to the erratically rhythmic pulse of the chit-chat in the shop since it was just as hard to watch TV in the chair in that you were chatting, spinning, and constantly adjusting your head per the barber's command. As an avid reader maybe my son would gravitate to the rack adorned with ancient *Sports Illustrated* magazines or maybe he would gaze at the shelf behind the barbers that was full of the tools the barbering trade—towels, scissors, clippers, and, of course, containers of the that waxy red gunk that barbers liberally apply to "flat top" cuts to make the hair stand perfectly upright as if cemented into place.

On the other hand, my son might focus on the people and not the things. Would he wonder what the waiting customers were thinking about as they stared straight ahead at strangers sitting in the barber chairs? Similarly, would he wonder what it would be like to sit in the chair and have strangers staring at him? Maybe he would notice that it was a virtually all-male environment, save the very occasional woman with kids in tow (divorced? husband out of town?). He was probably too young to observe that a barber shop is a great leveler of men; doctors and lawyers mingle equally with laborers and dishwashers, all beholden to the four men who had control over a most visible aspect of their appearance.

I didn't really have time to ask him because shortly after we sat down it was his turn. Here I made a fateful decision. Wilbert's chair was the open one, but I could opt, as per shop protocol, to wait for Ed's chair to open up as many of his loyal customers did or even wait for Roy or Forest. I rolled the dice and we went with Wilbert; again, what could go wrong? My son obediently climbed onto the board that barbers rest across the arms of the chair to raise children to a comfortable height for cutting their hair. It was at this point that my day started to veer from all my previous visualizations of the experience. Wilbert asked me if I wanted him to give my son a "regular" haircut. Inwardly I gasped as I realized that I had no idea what a "regular" haircut was; I had always given specific instructions to a barber, i.e. short in the back, no whitewalls around the ears and leave the sideburns. Outwardly, I mumbled some vague form of confirmation to Wilbert while chastising myself for my lack of preparedness—why had I not thought this through before?

That bumble though, paled in comparison to, or perhaps led to, the event that unfolded next: quite simply, Wilbert proceeded to give my son the single worst haircut that I've ever seen a professional barber give! There didn't seem to be any point at which adjacent hairs were cut to the same length; instead the ends of the hair that wrapped around his head resembled a crooked saw blade with teeth of random lengths. I was too aghast to say anything as Wilbert made it worse and worse. Had I been able to think I might have thought of Ralphie in *A Christmas Story* who eagerly awaited his visit with Santa but whose world suddenly and unexpectedly took a 180-degree turn when Santa turned out to be a mean man with bad breath who kicked him down the chute. Not being a barber, how could I tell Wilbert how to fix it? Were his glasses foggy? Did he need a new prescription? Could he possibly, somehow, be hungover? Mercifully, he finally stopped and introduced my son to that great barbershop tradition for kids of picking out a lollipop while I paid and—gulp—even tipped Wilbert.

My mind raced with trepidation as I headed home with my son, who was cheerfully unaware of my distress. How could I explain this to my wife? When we entered the living room where she sat on the couch eagerly awaiting our return, her reaction was swift and sure and has become a focal point of this story that has become solidly entrenched in our family lore: at first sight of our son she burst into tears of unhappy shock. I don't remember much about the next few minutes other than thinking about how I'd missed the mark in this ritual. Fortunately, rational thinking soon returned to both of us; it was, after all, just a haircut and our son could not have cared less. There was a change though; from then on she took him to a woman's stylist until he reached an age to take care of his barbering himself.

I, however, continue to patronize Ed's shop and I never said anything to Wilbert who, ironically, ended up giving me some of the best haircuts I ever got. He and Forest are retired now but Ed, at 85, is still there, albeit three days a week. It will be sad when he and the shop are gone, a special place with a special memory for our family.

Rituals

by Proal Heartwell

Life was full of rituals when I was growing up in Southside Virginia. There was the schoolday ritual of walking home for lunch, when Ruth, our family maid, paused in her ironing of my father's shirts to prepare for me a grilled cheese sandwich and a bowl of Campbell's Tomato Soup. There was the Sunday ritual of donning my acolyte robes at St. Andrew's Episcopal Church, lighting the altar candles, always working out from the cross, first right, then left. And of course, there was the summer ritual of Little League baseball and complicated, superstitious routines involving socks, stirrups, and the crease of the cap.

As a young boy, my most cherished ritual was accompanying my father on his Saturday morning errands downtown. First stop was the vaulted lobby of People's Bank and mysterious transactions at the counter. Often, Daddy would chat with cigar-smoking Frank Newsome, president of the bank and father of Pam, my contemporary who dazzled crowds (or at least me) as a junior majorette during halftime shows of the Brunswick High School football games. Next stop was the hardware and furniture store formerly owned by my grandfather. The business was sold after his death, but the family still owned the building and Father dutifully dispatched his duties as landlord. Then, it was on to the post office to procure stamps for the unceasing remittance of bills, bills that often elicited groans from my father as he worked in his home office off the downstairs hallway. Across the street from the post office sat the ABC store, where Daddy loyally procured a fifth of Jack Daniels, siphoned to make his nightly (just one) old-fashioned whose maraschino cherry I rescued and savored from the dregs of the finished drink. Stacking the shelves of the liquor store was Bradford Dillwyn, who on cold nights and early mornings stoked the coal furnace in our basement, the last such heater in town.

The highlight of these weekly excursions was a visit to Allen's Drug Store where Jessie Clary, mother of my friend Monk, concocted a chocolate shake for me and a malted milkshake for my dad. In the corner booth, he and I rehashed the the week's proceedings, lamented the poor play of our favorite baseball teams (Yankees for me, Giants for Daddy), and discussed plans for the amorphous future.

Once a month, our Saturday peregrinations also led us to City Barber Shop on Hicks Street. On these weekend mornings, this establishment transformed from a two-chair to three-chair business to better handle the additional influx of overall-clad farmers from the county, fresh from trips to the feed store or equipment shop. Probably many of you can picture the interior of City Barber Shop: the bay window, where boys like me played checkers; the lever-action barber chairs, with the strop for sharpening straight razors; the assorted outdoor and automotive magazines; the auto-parts calendar on the wall with a provocatively buxom blonde flouting her assets; the smell of Vitalis and talcum powder. This was a male world with male conversation: sports, politics, livestock, and the state of that year's tobacco crop. Occasionally, some unsuspecting mother dragged her son into the shop, and the men respectfully nodded their heads and conversation proceeded cautiously amid awkward pauses. When my turn in the chair was announced, I clambered onto the booster board and, as instructed, stoically kept my head still. Even so, once Wilson Elmore, the barber whose efforts my mother preferred, nicked my ear with his clippers and for not crying, I was rewarded with two lollipops instead of one at the haircut's conclusion.

At age 13, I went away to boarding school, and my rituals changed to embrace archaic traditions and rigid rules. These rules relaxed in time, and my hair grew longer in keeping with the fashion of the era. Haircuts were infrequent now and trips to the barber shop virtually non-existent. It could be that I trimmed my own hair or employed a dormmate for this purpose. Style was not important in this all-boys' environment, but it was essential to keep the hair out of your eyes while playing soccer or lacrosse.

When I matriculated at the University of Virginia, my long hair came with me. For awhile, I had my hair "styled" at Chateau Darlene on Wertland Street. Darlene was the first woman to cut my hair (other than my mother), and it took some time to develop a rapport with her. For some reason, Darlene had an arrangement with the University's athletic department, and lacrosse players got their hair cut for free. Now, I wasn't on the lacrosse team, which was one year removed from a national championship the year I entered UVa. I did try out for the team the fall of my first year with two other boarding school refugees. At the initial team meeting, all the "rookies" had to stand up and introduce themselves. There was much guffawing from the roster of Long Island and Baltimore natives as my friends and I announced we were from Danville, Virginia (Paul); Boyce, Virginia (Chip); and Lawrenceville, Virginia (me). After fall practice, the coach informed the three of us, "Well, I'm not going to cut you, but you'll never play." We decided that there were better ways to spend our time (i.e. girls and beer) and left the team. Still, I became friends with many lax players, which is probably why I went to Chateau Darlene (even though my haircuts were decidedly not free).

I spent the year after college in Southwest Virginia working for a citizens' environmental group helping people suffering property damage from irresponsible strip mining. The last few months there, I lived in George's Fork near Clintwood, the county seat of Dickinson County. In Clintwood, I got my hair cut for seventy-five cents from a kindly old man who had been barbering in the same one-chair shop for sixty years. Often, I took my meals at the diner around the corner where I feasted on meat loaf, green beans, and mashed potatoes for less than three dollars, tip included.

My first teaching job was at James Madison High School in Vienna, Virginia. A large suburban school, James Madison hosted extensive vocational classes, including cosmetology where teachers could get their hair cut for free. Mindful of my meager first-year teaching salary, I often took advantage of these "no cost" haircuts. However, after a few disastrous episodes, I deemed it best to let these future stylists practice on someone else's head.

I have now been back in Charlottesville for almost thirty years, and I've established a new ritual for barbering my gray hair, a ritual far removed from the male domain of my youth. You see, I am now a regular customer at Hair Cuttery, which I frequent on Saturday morning when the doors open at 8:00. I am greeted by Sherry, Nicole, Tonya, Bonnie, and Marqueta, and their talk is of children and the latest shenanigans of some misguided celebrity. Still, the conversation is warm and pleasant, in tone not unlike discussions of crop prices and animal husbandry I encountered at City Barber Shop in my youth. These ladies are efficient, and they do the best they can with my cow-lick hair. And, I bet if I were to ask, they would even give me a lollipop.

About the Contributors

Bahlmann Abbot, 62, is an architect in Charlottesville, Virginia.

Ed Banks, 52, is the founder of Corner Capital Management in Florham Park, New Jersey.

Jim Barns, 68, lives in Charlottesville, Virginia, where he is very successfully retired.

David W. Carr, Jr., 60, is General Counsel for the Southern Environmental Law Center in Charlottesville.

Sam Carr, 30, is a financial analyst for an investment firm in Charlottesville.

Jim Donahue, 74, is a retired military civil engineer living in Charlottesville.

Bill Dunnington, 64, is a management consultant in Colchester, Vermont.

Paul Erb, 59, teaches English at Woodberry Forest School in Madison County, Virginia.

Neal H. Gropen, 60, is a hunter-gatherer.

Proal Heartwell, 60, teaches English at Village School in Charlottesville.

Evans Humphreys, 11, is a student at Jack Jouett Middle School in Charlottesville.

Frank Kilgore, 62, is a lawyer, author, and retired mountain man in St. Paul, Virginia.

Dave Krovetz, 60, is a math teacher in Charlottesville.

Michael Kuchinski, 62, is a mathematics instructor at Germanna Community College in Fredericksburg, Virginia.

Bob Kusyk, 56, is the CEO of OESH Shoes in Charlottesville.

Gary Moody, 72, is in the computer support business in Charlottesville.

Gary Pelton, 58, is a clinical psychologist and clinical director at the Commonwealth Center for children and adolescents in Staunton, Virginia.

Corky Schoonover, 63, is a sales manager for Crutchfield in Charlottesville.

Cortlandt Schoonover, 28, is a computer programmer living in New Orleans, Louisiana.

Ken Wilson, 58, is a journalist and copyeditor in Charlottesville.

Francis Wood, 60, is a writer and the General Manager of WFLO AM/FM radio in Farmville, Virginia.

Tony Zentgraf, 61, teaches at Burley Middle School in Charlottesville.